Roadside
Loo
To Size 22

Sandra Matthews

Sheephouse Books

This book is dedicated to my Dad & Mam (John & Arlene Ryan). They instilled in me a love of learning and of respecting others, even those we disagree with.

Thanks again to Ciaran, April and Evan for their support and encouragement.

Copyright 2020 Sandra Matthews
IBSN: 9798696193243

Thank you for reading my book of poetry. This is a collection of poems, some written recently, others written many years ago.

I hope they speak to you.

Love Sandra

POETRY FOCUSES

Poetry focuses the heart
When mind has no idea where to
start

Let it in
A poem can lead you
On your very own adventure

POETRY IS

Poetry is odd
Author thinks they're God
Vomiting up words
To tickle reader's ear
Can't see yourself reading
Sipping favourite beer

OR

Poetry is hip
Takes us on a trip
Puts into words
The ups and downs we feel
Young and old are reading
Words can touch and heal

GRANNY

By the time I knew Granny
She was already old
Ancient
Wrinkled
Shoes flat and brown
Walking stick needed for trips
into town

By the time I knew Granny
I was already young
Active
Fresh-faced
Shoes high and white
Strutting my youth in town day or
night

Too young to read my Granny's
book
Too self-absorbed to listen or
look

Are generation gaps but cruel
Setting us up to be fools?
Carelessly we throw away
Wisdom elders share each day

Though I knew that Granny cried
In youthfulness I never tried
To understand how she might feel
A Granny's pain did not seem real

I would cherish her story now
Question, listen, ask her how
She carried on when life grew
cruel
Stayed sharp in wit
Never a fool

I cannot turn the clock around
Nor walk back over ancient
ground
Can't go back to hold her hand
Or learn to fully understand

Can generation gaps be kind?
Do young folk bring peace of
mind
To elders as they limp through life
Yet find relief from pain and strife

By focusing on our budding
throng
Energy high, passions strong
Loving life youth cheer folk on
Urging all to sing life's song

I hope that my self-centered
young way
Somehow cheered my Granny's
day

When expecting her to listen
Focus on me
Was life happening
As it's meant to be?

Her hair was white
Her shoes were brown
Her walking stick she brought to
town
By the time I knew Granny
She was already old
Just how many stories
Did those wrinkles hold?

SHIT SHIT SHIT

Beginning with sh and ending
with it
When I think of Granny
This word seems to fit

She would repeat and say it three
times
Heard her so often it stuck in my
mind

She had her set way
Granny's views could be strong
Yet such was her welcome
She helped us belong

You could call unannounced
Bringing a friend
Granny put on the kettle
All shyness would end

Tea in a cup
Not a big mug
Sugar of course
And milk in a jug

When we were children
Her pond drew us in
Teeming with gold fish
Too shallow to swim

But that did not stop us
From making a splash
With clothes dry and clean
To the pond we would dash

Beginning with sh
And ending with it
When I think of Granny
This word seems to fit

And if I could ask her
Is this poem a hit
My guess is she'd answer me
"Ah shit shit shit"

EASTER SUNDAY, CHOCOLATE FUNDAY

Visitors brought sweet treats
Which in Lent we could not eat
Mam would save them in a jar
Easter seemed sadly far
Tall glass temptress claiming
sweets
Piling higher with passing weeks

Easter eggs on mantlepiece
Calling us to early feast
Back of one egg we enjoyed
Tip toed off with spirits buoyed
Considered would folks notice
Lecture, scold and hotly roast us

Discovery of said crime
Protracted till Easter Day
Relieved to hear them laugh
Though we have no photograph
Fondly recall that Sunday
Happy kids on Chocolate Funday

ROADSIDE LOO

You may say I'm dreaming
But my bladder is small
Not able to hold
Much liquid at all

If I've been to your house
I've visited your loo
Two or three times
My words they are true

These days I can giggle
As a child it seemed cruel
Stopping to pee
Made me feel such a fool

I clearly remember
Being on a big bus
Teachers not happy
When I made a fuss

We were off on a school trip
When I knew I must go
Nuns told me to wait
But I replied NO

The driver pulled over
Others told not to look
No way, no way
This was one for the book

So, off the bus I hopped
This pee could not be stopped

Embarrassed
With nowhere to hide
Diluting
All remnants of pride

Giggling faces looked on
Row by laughing row

But when
You've got to go
You gotta go
You gotta go

HAVE ANOTHER APPLE

Remembering times of Saturday studying
Conscientious student
Bright eyed teen
Eating apples
More apples
Sure, have another one

They are good for me
Why not eat
And eat and eat

Belly swollen
No understanding then
Of mind messed on the study of food

Remembering days of bloated belly
Self-conscious girl
Insecure teen
Eating nothing
More nothing
Sure, have more nothing
Slimming's good for me
Why not try
And try and try

I was slim until bloat arrived
Just landed
Uninvited
Seemed outside of my control

Watched and stressed as tummy swelled
Wished and worried and willed it away
More I tried
Longer it would stay
Till it would somehow fade away
For days
Weeks
Of comfortable easiness

Fat not my companion
Freedom my for now friend
Till shadow of bloat returned
Unexpected
Never or rarely understood

Looking back now
I stretch out kindness
To that teen torn by food

Gluttony?
Yes
Self-idolatry?
Perhaps

Still I see not consuming
In deliberate greed
But snatchings of teen
In panicked need
Not yet grasping how food
Does not all hunger feed

JUST FRIENDS

They broke up
She ended it one lonely night
Deep cut
Her words tore through
Like sharpened knife

Stayed friends
Softer
Kinder
Seemed that way
Why not
Save precious friendship from decay

Years passed
She could sense his love still strong
Her new beaus
Came but never stayed for long

She could sense his love yet real
His new gals
She welcomed each with bleeding zeal
Beautiful yet wrong
They could not belong

A happy day at last arrived
Back together side by side
Learning they each felt the same
Starting out to try again

Months passed
Now she knew this was not right
Love but
Not the love of man and wife

Heartbreak
Love and friendship both now end
Tell me
Were they truly
Just friends?

MYOPIC

Whistling
He kept whistling
Ignored him
Yes, I turned away
But he it seemed was there to stay

Persistent
He just would not stop
As I was walking
Back from the shop

Determined he seemed
To catch my attention
Mumbled angrily under my breath
With words now best not mentioned

He clearly was in this to win
So, I dashed towards the office
To hurry on in

He caught up with me
I was not pleased
And all because I could not see

It was my boyfriend
Much amused
And glad to see I would refuse
Attention from others making passes
With or without myopic glasses

BIGGER IS BETTER

Roses are pink, yellow too
On Valentine's Day only red will do

All can see he loves you
Based on how much he has spent
Does he care enough to starve
Or delay the rent?

Bigger is better
Expensive is best
Pay close attention
To the annual love test

The roses, where did he buy them
Are they premium and fresh?
Not a last-minute purchase
On way home from gym sesh!

The date, how did he plan it
Did it clearly take much thought?
Does the theme match precisely
With the many gifts he bought?

The gifts, are they expensive
Do they show he knows you well?
Will it fill you with pride
To all your girlfriends tell?

The food. is it your favourite
Had he checked the menu first?
Do they serve your preferred beverage
To blissfully sate your thirst?

The setting, has it good lighting
Will it make a video clear?
Does he understand the need
For your fans to see and hear

How wonderful you are
Perfect is your life
Far removed are you
From loneliness or strife

Followers will watch
Wishing to be you
Loved up by a man
Who knows your value true

Roses are pink, yellow and black
Valentine's Day is no time to slack

FAKE TAN

My legs are pale and freckled
Bronzing not in their plan
Dare I wear dress
Showing such pallor
Or must I apply fake tan?

Tan is needed I thought
Packed bags and lotion brought
We were off to a summer wedding
Scenic spot by the sea
None would care how my legs looked
Still it mattered greatly to me

Got up early to give myself time
Dress was short
Tan must be sublime

When job was done
Felt chuffed
Impressed
So evenly applied
None would guess
Such tan to be a fake
Then came my foolish mistake

While rinsing hands
The water splashed
Over to the mirror dashed
Zigzags of pale shone through the brown
Looking like this I could not go down
Rescue attempt made it worse
Wanted to cry or scream or curse

It was time to leave
We could not delay
In panic I scrubbed
Washed tan away

My boyfriend told me
I looked very well
But through the day long
Felt sure all could tell

Kept trying to pull my skirt down
To cover the shameful white
Yet now if I had
Those legs gorgeous and slim
I'd be showing them off all night!

ST BRIGID'S DAY

St. Brigid's Day was Mam's birthday
A sentimental time each year
So too the remembered voice
Of my father in law I hear

St Brigid's Day is the first of Spring
We speak of hope while cold winds sting
Warm weather feels a world away
The first of February a bleak cold day

My father in law knew the land
When the Dublin girl
Could not understand
How Spring had sprung
Though nothing changed
No signs of seasons rearranged

He talked of growth beneath the ground
Stirrings of new life
With patience he explained such things
To his son's young wife

All I could see was cold
While growth was taking hold
Whispering first then shouting bold
Colours of green and yellow gold

Opening act, the daffodil
In gardens, parks and window sill
Tickling hearts with gentle thrills
Spring was prepping her bright new frills

FROM AVRIL TO APRIL

My daughter was born on New Year's Eve
Folk often find it hard to believe
When they hear her name is April

My daughter was born on New Year's Eve
She's even been asked
When was she conceived
All because her name Is April

My daughter was born
December thirty first
Yet April Fools' Day
Has often proved worst
Hearing the same joke for a millionth time
Wondering whether to curse or smile

Let me take you back to when I was a child
Visiting with a school friend of mine
(My age was eight or maybe nine)

My pal was called Avril
She was proud to explain
How a calendar month
Was the same as her name

This was exciting
Big news to digest
I was intrigued
Suitably impressed

From Avril to April
When changed into English
The name I loved
Both fresh and distinguished
There and then I would decide
How to name a female child

My daughter was born on New Year's Eve
All those years later I would still believe

Her name it must
Be April

STRETCH MARKS

When baby first arrived
She drew stretch marks on my heart
Pink and tiny bundle
Brought to us a fresh new start

When baby first came home
Her clothes dried on the landing
Pink and tiny signs
Of a family expanding

When baby settled in
Her every move we studied
Fascinated by this child
Whose glow could not be muddied

When baby called the shots
We would joyfully obey
Tending to her needs
Without question or delay

When baby woke at night
We would groan from lack of sleep
Yet through exhaustion's fog
We would still our promise keep

When baby captured us
She transformed our every dream
Considering her best life
Became part of plan or scheme

Now the line holds jerseys
Pegged up next to jeans
Washing her own clothes
Dreaming her own dreams

Those stretch marks on my heart
Will never fade away
This life of ever letting go
Is best lived day by day

PAINT ON A SMILE

She's my darling
So is he
When someone hurts them
They hurt me

Chest clamps tight and sore
I let myself expect more
Fool fool fool
Many times have I had
This conversation with myself
My ways are my ways
Don't expect them from anyone else

Tears bursting to flow
Not now
Please not now
Visitors due
Must hold tears back somehow

Why should I expect
Someone else to care?
Consider them
Or even be aware?
Logically I am being quite unfair

Tears flow
Sobbing
Heaving
Reason no more
My heart is grieving
Visitors thankfully are delayed
This little thing has me dismayed
There there enough of that
My logic and I we have a chat
The other person has a point of view
Now try hard to appreciate that

No use
No use
Who am I kidding?
Try to be noble
But tears are still winning

Visitors due in a very short while
Take out my make up
And paint on a smile

AUGUST THOUGHTS

When August comes round, I feel free
Knowing that soon September will come
And my children will stay home with me

Back to helping them work out their math
Ready for times when we just dance
Smiles for teddies who come to school
Tears when Mammy loses her cool

Days we laugh, days we fight
Days we're slow, days we're bright
Days we think till our brains hurt
Days we talk of silly stuff

Back to history books new and old
Ready for stories imagined and told
Smiles for art days with paint and brush
Tears of frustration when we rush

Days we chat, days we cry
Days we mess, days we try
Days we understand so much
Days we feel out of touch

Back to quiet moments of just us
Ready for lots of noise and fuss
Smiles for funny jokes and cuddles
Tears for days we're sad and troubled

Now that it's August I feel free
Knowing that soon September will come
And my children will stay home with me

FADED MONDAY

After weekend away
Monday feels grey
Slowly moving
Glad to be home
Not all alone
Phone is handy
But hugs delicious
Warm, smiling, spiced with mischief

What's in that bag?
What did you buy us?
From simple blue bag
Comes sweets and books
Cuddles, kisses, noise and fuss

After weekend away
Monday brings haze
Dragging heavy
I'm settled by nature
Love to come home
So why then does Monday bring
Slow hours
Faded colours
And birds that do not sing?

ULYSSES PROBABLY ABOVE MY HEAD

Met a poet this weekend
Who blessed me with her work

She paints pictures with words

Stirred by depth and truth
I read and read again

Honest raw emotions
Framed in faith
Hanging on the dado rail of motherhood
Kitchens, gardens and such things

Intimidated by her skill
I catch envy creeping in

Uncomfortable comparison
Some words I do not understand
And Ulysses probably above my head

Museums of art I have not seen
Tragedies of plays I have not grieved
Classics of opera I have not breathed

Stop
Stop that
Stop that now

Certificate in friendship
Tutored by my mother
Diploma in family business
Taught by Dad and my brothers
Degree in love filled marriage
Tutored by Mr. Right
Masters in cuddles and listening
Taught by children day and night

My poems must rise from deep in me
Not deep inside my dictionary

Prepare my work
To send her in the post
Remembering when we're truly ourselves
Is when we shine the most

And Ulysses, who's he when he's at home?

MEMORIES

Marshmallows in hot chocolate
Hold memories for me
Of a friend called Finola
Who showed me this recipe

It was sweet hot and delicious
When I was tired and cold
A group of us were camping
Some young and some not too old

Whenever I see marshmallows
I think of that camping café
Can almost taste the sweetness
As though I drank it but today

Finola has moved down the country
No longer lives in the big smoke
This memory keeps her with me
Though it's years since last we spoke

At the sound of a cawing. bird
I'm in Sandyford once again
With Granny's sugary breakfasts
The fish and dogs and hens

Grandparents have passed on now
No longer live up by the hill
This memory keeps them with me
Many years but I think of them still

Mysterious can be our memories
Though coloured and biased somehow
Often, I look at my children
Seeing them building memories now

ORDINARY DAYS

Milk in morning cuppa
Butter on my toast
Fruit for the juicer
Letters in the post

Kiddies' waves and kisses
As Daddy drives away
Breakfast fights and laughter
To start our humdrum day

Meat from the freezer
Potatoes on to roast
Books back to the library
Picking up their coats

TV after dinner
Children's time for bed
Sleepy hugs and chats
Favourite stories read

Flicking the channels
Too tired to use my head
The bookshelf looks inviting
But surfing wins instead

Another weekday ending
In an uninspiring way
But thank god for every
Precious Ordinary Day

PROPER TEA

To make a proper cup of tea
The water must be boiling
But oh, my friend, she did not know
So, on she kept a toiling

A slice of cake upon a plate
Soft seat for my behind
My dear sweet friend was hosting well
Loving me and being kind

When all things else were set in place
T'was now time to wet the tea
I tried, I did, I really tried
It was just too much for me

My hand reached for the kettle switch
To make water boil again
When bubbles were a leaping high
Then and only then

Did we make a true cup of tea
My friend was much amused
And when I visited again
She was no longer tea confused

HITS THE SPOT

Glass of water hits the spot
Cooler now
Not so hot

Pot of tea
Stirred not strong
Dreary day
Sings brighter song

Sip of merlot
Smooth and deep
With what ease
I could now sleep

A simple three
A complex me

When I thirst for one
The other will not do
Times when they can interchange
Are genuinely few

SMOKED EASTER HAM

A well-earned rest on the couch
Led me into a sleepy slouch

Deep, deep, I dropped
On cushions propped

Till all too soon abruptly woke
"Mam, the kitchen's filling with smoke"

At first, I did not understand
My mind still craving sleepy-land

Then "oh no, the ham" I cried
Mind no longer sleepily tired

Stumbled to the kitchen fast
Intent on saving our repast

When crispy edges shaved away
We saved the meat of the day

What a clever cook I am
I now know how to smoke a ham

FANCY STEWS

One Pot Wonders make my day
(Fancy stews, one might say)

How fabulous it feels
To have dinner organised
A simple thing like this
Is cause for joy and pride

Not for me the hassle
Of many pots and pans
Chuffed to have a dinner
That I actually planned

Tomorrow I may be
In pure chaotic mess
Today I shine my halo
Domestic Goddess

FART

Squeeze tight
You can do it
Hold
Until it passes

As you grip
Keep praying
That this
Motley stew of gasses

Is the sweetest kind
In silence leaks from one's behind

Then no one else need
Ever know nor mind

Unless you were to write
A poem confessing
In that case you're a lost cause
Too dumb to keep 'em guessing

MOST EMBARRASSING FART

T'was a cold winter's evening
When we gathered for dinner
Warm comforting chili
Always a winner

We then dispersed to various rooms
For study, TV or meetings on Zoom

When I noticed it brewing
Hoped 'twould easily pass
Discreet in the manner
Of ladylike gas

Accepted I then
This was not the case
Aimed but to hide
Panicked look from my face

Sought out the most remote
Part of the house
Safely away from
Offspring or spouse

Quickly I hurried there
Cheeks squeezing tight
Closed door and set free
Its thundering might

Sighed in relief
To have found a safe zone
Switched light on to find
I was not alone

He'd been silent in dark
And meditative space
Now he wore shock, horror
Over his face

NO KETCHUP

Ketchup
I do not like it
Never
Not at all

No matter what I'm eating
I'd never make the call
To flavour it with such a sauce
And need I say it makes me cross

When I order a burger
And they rarely understand
I want it plain
(Or with salad and mayo)
Please do not lay a hand

On that big red bottle
Please do not forget
When I said no ketchup
It's truly what I meant

RELATIVES ARE COMING

The relatives are coming around
Help from the kids cannot be found

They tell me to relax
Why must the house be clean
No one else will notice
Sure I'm just a drama queen

The bathroom is disastrous
They ask me who will care
I for one am freaked out
Don't want a judging stare

Not that anyone would say much
But I'd know what they'd be thinking:
What's happened to our sis
Her standards are surely sinking

So on I go with the cleaning
I'll have the place soon gleaming
My kids would not be rude
They will help to eat the food

SPRING CLEANING

Sweep, mop, wipe
Vacuum, shake and dust
Convention will say
Spring cleaning is a must

Get rid of clutter
Sponge down the walls
Shine till windows sparkle
Scrub until you fall

Exhausted into bed
Your hard work plain to see
Or
Write about it instead
Spring cleaning is not for me

MUCKY FLOORS

Never ending muck
Is a gift that keeps on giving
Reminding us to cherish
The sweet climate we live in

Drought a rarity
Except in summer hot
No luscious grass in Spain
They do not enjoy our rain
Taste of golden butter
Makes it worth the pain

These thoughts we keep in mind
As we count paw prints on the floor
Leading to the front
From the back door
Not even a suggestion
That we might think to roar
Or threaten that we cannot
Mop this any more

Our character is such
We'd not complain too much
Instead we call it lucky
To live with floors so mucky

CODE BROWN

Our dogs don't shed
They do need grooming
There was a time
When we were assuming

That we could save
With longer gaps between
Why groom often
Our lovely dogs are clean

Then came Code Brown
We could now understand
There are some things
Not meant for un-gloved hand

Code Brown happened
Poo stuck in matted hair
Long locks looked cute
But now we did not care

Off to the groomers
They regularly go
Code Brown free now
And relieved to tell you so

TINY VISITOR

Two adults and three bigger dogs
She would not let them pass
They'd arrived home
While she was eating in the hall
She was not budging
Never mind that she was small

Growling with a vicious tone
She would not let them in
They'd dared interrupt
Her precious dinner was at stake
She was not moving
Such commotion she did make

Mam quickly to the rescue
Amused by such a show
With some calming words
Lifted Dee and her dinner
Our visitor though small
In attitude a winner

RUGBY GIRL

Mouthguards are not pretty
These boots are not the sexy kind
Rain has ruined your make-up
Girl, this is not the look
Hunky guys have in mind

Rucks don't smell of roses
Scrumming spoiled your fresh sprayed tan
Mud has streaked your fair face
Girl, this is not the way
To find yourself a man

Mouthguards might protect you
From spouting your old school tosh
Sport has given me focus
Lady, I'm not trying
To be genteel or posh

There is more to my life
Than the stale gender trap
Of living to impress
A fine handsome chap

GOOD IMPRESSIONS

Make a good impression
That is what they say
But have you noticed it will be the day
When you are looking rushed and ruffled
Then it's likely you'll be troubled
With meeting people
(Who fall out of bed looking well)
While you are feeling like an extra
For shows about dark days in hell

When our kids were still in class
I would dress smart and neat
For visiting their school
When teachers we would meet

Then one day they called
From cinema with school trip
Could I please collect
Could I drive with my hip?

Had been resting on couch
My back sore and tight
Still to help my sweet dears
Seemed the path right

To Dundrum I go
Wearing tracksuit and sloppy hair
Happy in my plan
To hide in car when I get there

But teacher would not
Let them loose
So now I had no excuse

Walked through mall looking a state
Believe me I do not exaggerate

Yes, make a good impression
Never let your standards slip
Not even when you're home on couch
Resting with sore hip

Or sod it
Hold your head up
Some things matter more
Impressions are important
But who is keeping score?

TALK TO YOURSELF

Talking to yourself
Is the first sign of madness
Especially so if you answer back

Where did that knowledge come from?
To me it seems way off track

I've talked to myself for years, nay more
It helps me to work through
Project and chore
And when I'm feeling tired and sore
There's nary a one
Would be interested more

Talking to yourself
Is a sign of sanity
Especially so if you
Speak much sense
Let us now share this knowledge
Please do not sit on the fence

I've talked to myself for years, nay more
I'm sure it would help you
In plan and chore
And when you are feeling sad or low
You'll now know with confidence
Where you should go

PLEASE MAM

Please Mam
Please
Pretty please
My keys are in the house

I rushed out this morning
So I would not miss the bus
I don't know what to do
I'm stressed out by this fuss

Please Mam
Please
Pretty please
I need my keys right now

I thought you'd be at home
So that you could let me in
I don't know what to do
I simply cannot win

Please Mam
Please
Pretty please
I'll bring my keys next time

I need you to come home
So I can change my bags
I don't know what to do
I can't go in these rags

Please Mam
Please
Pretty please
Your friends will understand

Sure aren't you always saying
We should lend a helping hand

MAM'S DOWNSTAIRS

Mam sits on the couch
Turns on her favourite show
Message spreads
Fast and wide
"Mam's downstairs, go, go, go"

Race to join her there
Pause that silly show
Share your cares
Deep and true
Mam will listen, we all know

Mam may look well rested
Sitting there alone
But she needs
Us to save her
From this mindless TV zone

GUILTY

Time to read a book
Or watch morning TV
Feel a little guilty
As if I should not be

Sitting on my bum
While around me
There is mess

Never ending laundry
And the hem
On my daughter's dress

Needs to be mended
If I can remember how
Sewing is a task that
Brings sweat beads to my brow

Time to cook the dinner
Serve up menu suave
Feel a little guilty
As if I should not have

Sat and read that book
Or watched that silly show
Now it's almost six
And my progress is too slow

Need to be speeding
If I can remember how
Cooking is a task that
Brings furrows to my brow

Dinner won't be ready
And I'm feeling hot and cross
Try to catch my breath
And take the pressure off

My own fault for reading
And watching some TV
Soon loved ones will be home
And the mess still clear to see

PANCAKE TUESDAY

Throw some flour in a bowl
Please don't ask "how much?"
A pinch of salt and sugar
No need for recipe crutch

Make a dent in the flour
Break eggs and pour them in
So easy peasy to make
Buying pancakes is a sin

Not the serious kind
That might land you in hell
Punishment is but in flavour
Shop bought never taste as well

Now add some milk
Mix and watch it blend
Let it rest in fridge awhile
Fry later and watch taste buds smile

WINTER BY ANOTHER NAME

Early Spring in Ireland
Winter by another name
Promise of change reassures us
While temperatures stay the same

Rain spits down upon us
Bitter, cold and sharp
Summer seems impossibly far
Clutching scarves tight
We dash to the car

Shivering, thawing
In out of the breeze
Rain falls to sleet
Roads race to freeze

Nothingness looms
Nothingness booms

Why call it Spring
While ice holds such sting?
Why build this season's claim to fame
When it is but winter by another name?

MOCK EXAMS

Mock Exams
Sent to focus minds
Time to set distractions aside

Real exams
Rolling fast towards June
Time to grasp it's happening soon

Then you'll pour out years
Fill your papers full

Spill cramming
Mix logic
While memory must not dull

Life exams
Toughest lessons yet

Time comes when
School results you will forget

EMBARRASSING BEST

When embarrassing your children
Do it with style
Trying to look cool
May work once in awhile
But it's generally a waste
Of your over stretched time

It is part of your job description
To regularly make them cringe
And with surprisingly little effort
You may earn the title "unhinged"

To this day I can remember
A slow song at a disco
With a chap I rather liked
And wanted to impress
When Dear Dad's interruptions
Tossed my plans into a mess

DJ's loud clear voice
Had me aghast
"Sandra Ryan, your Dad's at the door
And wants to get home fast!"

So, remember it's your job
Step up and pass the test
Your kids deserve to see
Your embarrassing best

ONLY A BUNNY

We lost three bunnies last year
Whispered good-bye to each cutie dear

The first was a shock
Healthy one day
Gone the next

Had hidden himself
As if sensed he would die
Only a bunny
Yet our eyes leaked to cry

Second was jarring
Out of the blue
Attacked

A violent clash
Though vets tried, she still died
Only a bunny
Yet our hearts sorely cried

By the third we were raw
Wearily warn
Resigned

Another farewell
Good byeing without end
Only a bunny
Or family and friend?

We lost three bunnies last year
Each one different
Each one dear

ARE RESULTS IN YET

Waiting to see the doctor
Are results in yet?

Learning to be patient
Aiming to forget

How his few words
Might shape our future years
Medical jargon clogging our brains
Bringing us joy or tears

Waiting to see the doctor
Can we turn back time?

Learning to appreciate
Aiming to divine

How our few prayers
May guard us in this plight
Emotional jargon flooding our thoughts
With sentiment day and night

Waiting to see the doctor
Putting our lives on hold

Learning to survive
Aiming not to scold
How daily life carries on regardless
Meaningless jargon tiring our minds
With matters we deem pointless

Waiting to see the doctor
Are results in yet?

Learning to be grateful
Aiming to accept
How simple kindness blesses limbo days
Family jargon soothing our hearts
And friends who are not afraid

HER NAME

Why do people fight off pain
Every time I say her name?

Why such need to cheer me up
As if I were a child in sulk?

Why convince me she's now free
As if that's truth I cannot see?

Yes, yes indeed, I held on tight
Wished her well with all my might

Was that because I loved her so
Or needed her love?

I don't know

I do know
She was always there
From baby steps
To brushing hair

Loving me
And my kids too
A mother's heart
Loyal and true

So even if it flickers pain
Do not protect me from her name

HER LAST MOTHER'S DAY

Her voice no longer sounded
Like her own

Medication mixed with pain
Had changed how she would
Say my name

Her eyes no longer danced
With mischief bright

Treatments meant to heal and save
Had robbed from her
Though hope they gave

Mam wanted new pajamas
Could not find a pair of choice
Till she got a recommendation
Then phoned me
In her strange Mam voice

Wanted them for Mother's Day
Seemed pleased when I brought them in
My sister-in-law served a thoughtful cake
Mam did her best to grin

Weeks later we said our last good-byes
To her voice
Her smile
Her care

Mother's Day came around again
But Mam was no longer there

LOSS

Loss
Never fully goes away
Instead
We learn to greet it
Day
By day
By day
Carrying it with us
As we laugh
Work
Play
Its heaviness may vary
But far it will not stray

WINTER FUNERAL

By graveside
Raw cold winter day
Sending a loved one on their way

Tears of goodbye
Freezing to our face
Desolate is this wretched place

Season of death
Nature falls apart
Echoing pangs of broken hearts

SEASONS

Told me she missed the seasons

Had moved from Chicago
To live in L.A.
Where sunshine ever came to play
Day after day after day

Her words come to me often

When catch myself wishing for
Days ever clear
For we see not the value dear
Till something is no longer here

GOOD BYE

She'll be there to spend the winter
And many winters more
Has sold her house
Packed her bags
For life on Canada's shores

Friendship is a wonder
A joy
A pain
A leap
We let ourselves be open
Yet friends
Can
Never
Keep
A reign on freedom's call

I'm just home from the airport run
Time alone to let tears cry
She has been my friend
Just three years
But it's still hard to say goodbye

FIRELIGHT

Loneliness stung sharpest at the weekend
Kids do their own thing
No longer hide in mother's wing

Firelight is the bright spark of company
That sat and warmed me
Through that hollow time
Never rushed away
Or cancelled on the day
Its attention ever fully mine

Loneliness no longer calls so often
Sweeter now is life
Flavoured with ordinary strife

Firelight is still a cherished visitor
Sits and warms me
Happy here to dwell
Asks that I feed it
There when I need it
Warms my soul to see its sparkling spell

THEY DID THEIR BEST

They did their best
The whoever people
Who stamped their words onto our
Childhood days
Cared
Loved
Shaped our ways

Looking back, we catch the lies
Spoken truthfully
Tinting our eyes
To see as they saw

They
Scarred by their whoever people
Stamped into us
Impressions long inherited

We travel on with carvings ingrained
Descriptions
Perceptions
Presumed to be true
Time embedded them deep
In our marrow they grew

Express old stuff they say
They who counsel us towards freedom
Let it out
But how?
When our pourings deluge
Onto they who have loved
Or swamp our memories
With harshness of truth

Hushed feelings awake
Tummy tenses tight
No sweeping brush of logic
Can hide their mess from sight

Anger hidden in crevice dark
Resentments shooting
From the rotting guilt
Cross at being cross
What right have we to anger?

Loved
Blessed
Cherished
No place for
Murky stomach cramps of thought

Can we dare to let emotion flow?
Safe to know
Reflection will not fall
On they who loved and gave their all?

Express old stuff they say
As if it were a simple thing to do

MENOPAUSAL MARY

Menopausal Mary is my name
Well no, it's not
But when I'm hot
(And not the sexy kind)
My dearest darlings find
That Menopausal Mary
Says a lot with just two words
And maybe helps them feel
Their voices have been heard

When they come home
From a day at work or school
To a house with temperatures
"Baltic" as a rule
They keep hats and coats on
While I wear jeans and shirt
Rub their hands together
And talk of how it hurts

Indoor climate almost scary
When thermostat controlled
By Menopausal Mary

AULD WAN

Menopause matters to auld wans
When did I join that throng?
Youth seems but a blip ago
Ageing feels weirdly wrong

Yes, it's a blessing
Living to this age
But thankfulness was tough
While surfing hormonal rage

When rage said goodbye
Daily teariness came
Sentimental Sandra
Was my temporary name

Then hot flushes started
Though less now
They're still here
Arriving unpredictably
Lest I lose the fear
Of they and their ways
Heating nights and days

Now I am an auld one
Somedays I feel it more
When dressing in layer
Upon many layer
Seems weary wardrobe chore

REPEAT

Cardigan on
Cardigan off
Repeat
Repeat
Repeat

Impossible to be discreet
While dealing with internal heat

Jacket on
Jacket off
And on
And off
And on

Tried diet, herbs, the list is long
The weaker sex is bravely strong

CANDLE RAGE

A candle was moved
From right place to wrong
My reaction came not as
A sweet caring song
But the roar of a bear
Scattering throng
Demanding said candle
Go where it belongs

No one was frightened more than I
And when the bear silenced
I started to cry
And cry
And cry
Asking why
And where had that come from
And how was I to carry on
Not knowing would I turn a page
And therein find again such rage

Mama Bear had visited before
Triggered by hurt or insult
To the children I adore
That made sense
A primal form of maternal defense

But a candle?

I TURNED AROUND

I turned around
That's all
No leap or fall or careless climb

Stuck
Right
There
Beside
Checkout
Counter

Nothing would help
At all
Spasm would pass in its own good time

Kids
Were
Wishing
The
Ground
Would
Open

OUCHY

Ow, that hurts
Ooh, I'm stiff
Slow down and wait for me

Hobbling for a moment
Until I get my stride
Trying hard to keep up
When walking by her side

Standing up from sitting long
My friends and I now sing a song
Of achy here and ouchy there
Appointments with physios
We compare

Youth may make more noise
As their music blares around
We just stand up from the couch
And make old people sounds

Ooh ow aaah
Need to slowly stand
Please lend me your hand

SCALES

The scales made no sense this morning
Threw me with number displayed
Cadburys may close
Due to loss of my business
Screen did not show that
I sank dismayed

One pound gained
Surely did not matter
One pound gained
Amplified mental chatter
Told me I was
Getting fatter and fatter

Stop!
No way am I listening to that
The scales are my helper
When I am their master
Loss of wise balance
Leads to disaster

I am more than my size
I have value regardless
Life is for living
Not just reaching targets

SIZE 22

Size twenty-two
With a wardrobe full
Of clothes that fit
Does not claim to heal the hit
Of pain
From chocolate binge
Or weighty gain
Instead they call my name
Shield me from the shame
Of too tightness
Or the zip of stress
A wardrobe victory
Soothes and comforts me

BATTLE OF THE BINGE

Wish I had not eaten that
Sweetness settling now to fat
Tummy swells
Mind dwells
Judgement knells

Be kind
Find grace
Let freedom flow

Battle of the binge
Wreckage brings
Fan hope alive
Till freedom sings

STARVE

Food gives us heat
Without it we'd be cold

And though they say we need less
As we gracefully grow old

The experts here are wrong
They cannot be right

I'm still prone to hunger
Of a cold winter night

And though my jeans are tight
I must keep myself fueled

To starve a person of my age
Seems a step too cruel

TOO MUCH

Welcome, warm welcome
To Calamity Jane
I'm so sorry for leaving you
Out in the rain
Embarrassed
Lest others might know your name
And guess how closely we are related
Old stories of childhood
Are now outdated
Only mentioned now and again
While I defiantly strive to explain
How we are no longer friends
My calamity days came to an end
How I left you behind
No more you and I
As my life sped on by

That's the same story I've told myself
As I've hidden you deep
In the back of the shelf
Behind tins of beans or stacks of delph
Tall piles of chocolate bars
Or giant packs of magic stars
Scheming but to keep you far
Away from me

So none could see
How much
I am too much
If I come out about you
If I am true
To who I am with you

So please forgive me Calamity Jane
It's taken too long
But now at last it's plain
That I sing my best song
Of melodic refrain
In harmony with one
I will no longer shame
Learning to be proud
When together
we are bravely loud

In the fullness of fun
Or formidable fear
In a life that is not
For the tame or faint-hearted
You and I Calamity
Sure, we're just getting started

SANCYCOVE SWIM

Sunshine on my shoulders
View across the bay
Pristine exhilaration
Midst an ordinary day

Gloves keep my hands warm
Ice shock fades away
Sparkling exuberance
Splashes dullness into spray

Wrapped in silky waters
Grown up child at play
Impossible feels possible
Tension drifts away

Bouncing with the waves
Gentle pull and sway
Pausing expectations
Of productive adult day

SANDYCOVE POST SWIM

Warm
Glowing
Proud
Drying, dressing, no rush at all
Watching the swimmers, I sit on the wall
Sense of achievement never goes away
Decide to come here everyday
Never mind the weather
I'm committing to forever
(Said promise fades away
When consider bleak harsh winter day)
For now, I sense no limitation
Belonging springs sure elation
Warm
Glowing
Proud
Tempted to shout this feeling aloud

EBB AND FLOW (Lockdown)

Sitting by water as it splashes my feet
Then dips back into retreat
Ebb and flow
Things come and go
Today I'm feeling sad
Someone I have had
Close to me
Will now be
Stepping out into a normal day
I've grown used to living this strange way
Family here so much
Their banter, noise and touch
Could truly be annoying
Yet I found myself enjoying
Their presence in laughter and stress
Real life comes in sunshine and mess
Now as we start to unfurl in stages slow
Life splashes us
Bitter sweet its ebb and flow

RHYTHMS

Year after year we grow used
To a pattern and rhythm of life

Sense of normality comforts
Lowers levels of stress and strife

Routines may seem unimportant
Indeed, they are anything but

When things happen as they are meant to
It feels right deep down to our gut

FEELINGS

Feelings knock us over
Grab our guts and punch
Leaping out of nowhere
Reeling into lurch

Smile
Look happy
Pretend all is well

No, no no
No
Do not that
Version tell

RAW

How are you today?

I'm raw
Sore
Bruised
In hidden places
Feeling off
Not sure why

Are you sorry you asked
Have you been shaken by honest reply?

GREEN GRASS

Your grass grows luscious green
To they who see it from the other side

Kick shoes off
Sense warm earth
Stretch toes lazily wide

Bow not to guilt
Hold head high
They see not your pain
Nor silent cry

SILENCE SHOUTS

Silence shouts
We shut it out
Silence screams
"Listen please"

Silence turns volume up
So, we hide in screen or cup

Run toward need
To be freed
Of niggling thoughts
That cut and bleed
In search of noise
This quest will lead

Silence shouts
We block it out

FALL

Fell the other day
Nothing broken
Hairline fracture
To the notions of immortality

That hide
Where the mind
Smuggles in delusion

Invincibility is illusion
Vulnerability is fact

WOUNDED

Wounded and wondering
When will I win
The gift of caring not

Wounded and suffering
Crafting to shape
The shield of bullet proof

Wounded and filtering
Pain that I can
Or cannot control

Wounded and learning that
All I can do
Is be and let it be

WINTER BLUES

Winter blues blend with January greys
On a palette of dull and dreary days

Black clouds squashing heavily
Frowning, leaning down on me
Want to lift them, fling them far
So I can clearly see a star
Or the sun
Or an icy sky of blue
Something other than greying doom

Winter blues blend with January greys
On a vista of dark and gloomy haze

Short days squeezing energy
Yawning, draining life from me
Want to stretch them, give them light
So I can clearly see at night
Sky of blue
And a sun of yellow
Something feeling warm and mellow

Winter blues blend with January greys
On a season of long and lonely days

WOULD I TELL HER

Usually love to be alone
Now I long for the telephone
To ring and a friendly voice to ask
"How have you been since I saw you last?"

Would I tell her
There is so much on my heart
That I never seem to know
Quite where to start?

We would chat about silly things
Trifles and news each season brings
We would laugh about this and that
Saying little but loving the chat

Would I tell her
I'm too busy to see friends
Worn and spent out
When the day draws to an end?

We would chat about deeper things
Challenges that each season brings
We would talk about highs and lows
Busy days watching families grow

Would I tell her
The dark days make me sad
Even question if perhaps I'm going mad?

SCISSORS & HIGH PLACES

Scissors in the bedroom
No, no, no
Could not sleep
Lest I awake and cut

What or whom I did not know
Scissors
Scissors had to go

Sitting in high places
No, no, no
Could not rest
Lest I throw myself off

Why or when I did not know
Heights were
Places not to go

Years, years, years
I lived that way
Thoughts might threaten night or day

Knew I'd never do these things
And still they kept me on a string
Of jagged chaffing endless thread
Pulling tightest at night in bed

Postnatal depression
Dull yet sharp
Gripped my mind
Triggered obsessions dark

Where to run I did not know
Thoughts
These thoughts had to go

Fears, fears, fears
Did blight my way
Till freedom called then came to stay

Severing the string of dread
No jagged pull of chaffing thread
Can keep me now
Not even in bed

WE STILL HAVE TREES

Motivation dashed away
"What's the point?" came to stay
Truths needing to be heard
Lost in maze of miserableness

We still have trees
Standing, swaying, silently blessing
Here before me
Here after me

Cheeriness raced away
Sad and lonely called to stay
Dullness clouds heavy day
Caught in daze of miserableness

We still have trees
Standing, swaying, silently blessing
Here before me
Here after me

Catch myself in fantasies of escape
Could slip away for unplanned break
Leave pressures, questions, obligations
Life of pin pricks and frustrations

Rest, silence, ease
Might set me free
Only problem is
I would have to go with me

We still have trees
Standing, swaying, silently blessing
Here before me
Here after me

We still have trees.

HILLS

Sublime in storm or breeze
Hills care not who they please

They meditate on now
Inviting us to bow

Low
Till worries fall into ease

ONE LIGHT MATTERS

Brightness in the dark
Gifting us a spark
Of hope
Of cheer
Of respite from fear

One light matters
One flower catches a heart
One soft petal
Breaks hard metal
Of cynicism
As praise dissolving criticism
One light can do
One me
One you

IT'S ALL G

It's all good
You can only do what you can only do
Beyond that is beyond you

Today you can or cannot
All you can give is what you've got

Then sit back and say
I did my best today

It's all G

A GRAND STRETCH

There's a grand stretch in the evenings
Darkness is in retreat
Brightness shyly coaching us
Back out onto the street

Pale new light in timidness glows
We wait and watch
As her confidence grows
Week by week she gathers strength
Till day wins victory in its length

Night crawls back into his box
Puts on cap and pulls up socks
Alone in his dark and hidden ways
He dreams of returning darker days

I for sure will miss him not
Happy to see light take his spot

SURPRISES

Spring surprises us
With glimpses of light
Clusters of daffodils
Daydreams fresh and new

Oh, the things we will now do
With winter gone
Places we will visit
With bright days long

Stretching out of our cobwebs
We plan
Because we can
With hours of natural light
Fueling our will to fight
For a life of vision and goals
Doing things that feed our souls
No longer trapped in pigeon holes

The real me, the real you
Doing things we were born to do
When Spring comes with surprises new

GOING ANYWHERE NICE?

Are you going anywhere nice?
Never mind the price

Spring has sprung
Holiday ads have begun

You will see them everywhere
Whispering to your wish
To escape dull daily care

Book early
Special offers
Bag a bargain low cost
Daydreams drift down desert dunes
Far from the bite of frost

Are you going anywhere nice?
Great deals going on flights

Spring has sprung
Holiday ads have begun

Sometimes staycations must do
Yet ads build a magical fantasy for you

Are you going anywhere sunny?
Best way to spend your money

Early bird taking a leap
Pausing not to ask how
Future you can work and pay
Feels so right to book it now

SUMMER POSSIBILITIES

Time to believe
In outings we conceive
We will do much
We really will
We surely will

On days we actually do
We said we would
And followed through
Righteousness thrills our satisfied souls
Glowing pride of reaching goals

Declare we then to future self
All days will be as this
Grasping opportunity
Building summer bliss

Most days our energy
Reaches but to dreams
Summer's window never
As wide as it first seems

We find not oomph
To walk, swim, climb
Phone friends or
Gather for quality time

Summer days tinged with guilt
Opportunities recklessly missed

We could have
We should have
We will, we will

Maybe
Maybe not

If the garden chair
Is where adventures lead us
We will breathe in that air
Sip beverage free of fuss
Joy of doing nothing
Summer's gift to us

DOING NOTHING

Sweetness of doing nothing

Guilt calls to check your to-do list
And you laugh

Sweetness of doing nothing

Rest calls to check your to-be list
And you smile

Sweetness of doing nothing

AIRBNB

Chairs and sofas formed to them
Their pillows
Their sheets
Their shops and local streets

Their neighbours pottering
In ruts long laid
Their ordinary
The place where we have paid
To stay
On our much longed-for getaway

Someone else's suburbs
Someone else's keys
Another person's duvet
Another's TV screen

Someone else's balcony
Overlooking their local park
Where lurking in the dark
Of subconscious mind
Unsettled there I find

Longings for familiar
Ordinary
Mundane
Yearning for ruts of me and mine
Ploddings that change not much with time

Our Dublin streets
Where we walk three dogs
Our open fire
Where we pile chopped logs
Our neighbours
Who hold a set of keys
Our shops and park
Our local trees

Conscious mind excited
Holidays are fun
Seeing new sights
Eating out
Freedom to travel and roam

Still never can I fully squash
That whispered pull
Towards life back home

FLYING

Somehow suspended up in the sky
As if it is normal for humans to fly
I try to forget we are soaring so high
Look for distractions to pass the time by

As we are speeding six miles high
Or so the captain just told us
What is there to hold us

Rather than needing
To know how this works
Flee to escape in my new airport book
Pages of crispness
Overpriced
Priceless
Losing and finding myself in its niceness

Niceness? Really?
Too fidgety to care
While eternal skies lie under my chair

A SNORING MUM

Blame it on the strange bed
Or on the stress of travel
For when we grew tired
And wanted sleep
Such plans did quite unravel

Oh, not for me
I slept soundly
Same cannot be said
For those living around me

Was it triggered by holiday dining
Enjoying different food?
When it came to morning
Others were in sleepy mood

Oh no, not me
I slept soundly
Same cannot be said
For those living around me

With night time snorting
I serenaded
Varying from low to high
They were mostly polite
But I fear that by night
I made them want to cry

Not me of course
I slept soundly
Same cannot be said
For those living around me

After a few nights it stopped
We were all much elated
Still the question hangs
When we travel again
Will Mum's snoring be reinstated?

CONNEMARA COTTAGE

Wilds of Connemara
Cottage by the water
No need to cater for adult son or daughter
Just us two (plus dogs in tow)
Kids would complain that internet's slow
Weather changing by the hour
Sunshine playing chase with shower
Swimming togs, sweater, rain mac
Sandwiches and water in haversack
Beaches to find
Pubs to frequent
Sweet air to breathe is heaven sent

A week of nothing much to do
Preciousness of days with only you
And me
And us
Free of fuss
Jewels of quiet
Pearls of time to discuss
Past and future, how the years fly
Or merits of cream on apple pie
Eating too much
Though we said we wouldn't
Fresh food, so delicious
Resist it we couldn't

Lighting a fire as each evening takes chill
Our home for a week
Close by sea, field and hill
A movie to watch
Or a series to follow
Or sitting in silence never feels hollow
Me reading or writing
You making plans
Still being each other's number one fans.
No one can annoy me quite like you do
Yet through it all our old love is true

Writing this poem springs tears to my eyes
Knowing life brings hellos and goodbyes
Sentiment catches me, these days will pass
Our loves and dreams are fragile as glass

Back to the moment, I breathe in the bliss
Days do not come much better than this
Woman savouring
What life has brought her
Week in Connemara
Cottage by the water

PARKING BUSES

When I'm told there's space for buses
But believe my car won't fit
Men have come to my rescue
Amused by my driving skit

"Yi'd get a bus through there luv
C'mon yi'll be just grand"
And smiling with amusement
He directs with waving hand

Other men have exploded
Fuming as I tarry
Nervously freezing under stares
From Tom, Dick or Harry

Loudly beeping on the horn
Seething with impatience
He's asking "How much longer
Will this woman keep me waiting"?

So

When faced with smaller spaces
Yes, I'm prone to make a fuss
But these men would run in terror
If I tried to park a bus

DISORIENTATION

You may read this with amusement
But will you understand?

That depends on whether
You've experienced first-hand
The panic, almost terror
Of losing your way
The disorientation
Of going astray

I can get lost with scary ease
And feel like such a fool
Best if I can relax
To focus on using tools

The panic, almost terror
Of losing your way
The disorientation
Of going astray

You may give the best directions
My mind cannot compute
I may cause you frustration
As I'm otherwise astute

The panic, almost terror
Of losing your way
Please bring patience, not anger
If you find me this way

CAR PARK SEARCH

My case and I were ready to go home
As ladies hugged goodbye
Saying we must try
To get away together more often
My case and I were ready to go home
To the carpark now
Happy to know how
To find the way back to my Dublin town
My case and I were ready to go home
Headed towards my car
Glad it was not far
This hotel had carpark underground

My case and I decided we should part
Half an hour had gone
The search must go on
For car was hiding
Nowhere to be seen

My case understood she was too heavy
Alone I would be quick
This should do the trick
With car found
I would come back to collect

I found my car
I found my car
At last
Now to get my case
Just a simple race
Off to home we could now go together

Where was my case
Where was my case?
Oh no!
Tears began to flow
Simply did not know
How it had now vanished from my view

On and on this went
My emotions spent
Round and round I'd drive
Feeling panic rise
Knowing that I'd really need
To relax and deeply breathe
Would I ever leave this place
Or be doomed to drive in circles
Ever searching for a case

There it was
There it was
Relief!
I wonder if the reader thinks
This tale beyond belief

It is true
It is true
Though I wish it were not
For my sense of direction
You could never call hot

LOVE NOURISHES

Love
In its many sizes
Multiple guises
Brings painful shocks
And glorious sweet surprises

Love
Protects us from our greed
Loss brings painful bleed
Hide though we may
Love's nourishment
We ever need

FAMILY & FRIENDS

They make us laugh and cry
They help us to belong

They joke with us
(Or smoke with us)
Scaling harmonies in life's song

Loving us
When we do right or wrong

COMFORTABLE FRIENDS

Comfortable friends
Worn
Baggy fit
Keeping us warm
Covered
They who match
With anything we say or do

Comfortable friends
Laugh
Or ugly cry
One size fits all
Stretching to shape we are
Not size we hope or wish to be

In low key
High value way
They complement
Have their say

Comfortable friends
Everyone needs some in their wardrobe

CRAFTING FRIENDS

My craft room hidden
Under bead, scrap, flower
In need of quick tidy
Before morning shower

Tidied yesterday's papers
Glues, cutting mat
So busily sorting
Forgot about tap

Kettle filling for morning cup
Became fountain spilling
Must then be cleaned up

Water flowing onto kitchen floor
Splashed from the sink
With voluminous pour

Friends on their way
I'm busy with mop
By now I had planned
To be at the shop

Cake or biscuits
Must be gluten free
To serve to my pals
With coffee or tea

Opened the door
Still in dressing gown
This made them smile
No hint of a frown

Brought their own biscuits
Thoughtful indeed
They were happy to chill
No need for speed

They each created
With style and flare
Made it look easy
Yet finished with care

Laughed till our sides hurt
Serious fun
Craft brings together
The old and the young

LOVE, ACCORDING TO BEA

My friend
In love
Her face alight
The early days when fresh delight
Shows up for every call or date
And too long is the dragging wait
Till lovers meet again

My friend
Who knows
That I am there
To listen well and ever care
Show up in love yet set her free
As she has often done for me
Friends through high and low

My friend
Who knew me well enough
To see this time it would be tough
Her love though new
Was growing strong
We'd learned the Bible
Says that's wrong
Her lovers name was Bea

And Bea
She found it odd
This talk of God
She had not marinated
In the juices of scripture
As my friend or I had done
She'd travelled longer on a journey
We had just begun

And me
Mind fumbled
Structure crumbled
Liberal had been a word
To speak of faith untrue
Declaring truth as suited you
So began my search
For understanding right and true

A view of love too narrow
I slowly laid to rest
When scrutinized
These ancient ways
Could not pass love's test
By the grace of God
Whoever God may be
I breathed a sigh and now could see
The beauty of love according to Bea

IN HER SHOES

Knife fell
He stooped to catch
Knife caught him

Pumping red pinkie
Oozing gore
Knife unharmed
Finger scarred

And I
I looked away

Helping yes
Looking no
Oh, I could feel it
From head to toe

Legs weakening
Stomach curdling
And I
I looked away

Am I looking away now?
Her shoes bursting blisters
Watery or red
While I rest my gaze
On pleasant things instead

Am I looking away now?
Her shoes too small for growing feet
While I buy new sandals
For a treat

Am I looking away now?
Or staring without seeing
For unless I wear her shoes
I don't know how she's feeling

AGNOSTIC

My faith has fallen apart
Bringing freedom
Served with loss

My sureness days I miss
Not now knowing
What to think
About the Cross

SKY LOOKS SMALL

Through leaves and flowers
Sky looks small
Expanse hidden in plants tall

Willingly we grasp assumptions
Sweet presumptions

Dig roots into that garden
Seeds of conviction harden

Each one holding flowers
Larger than sky

THE OBVIOUS

If it goes without saying
There's a lot to be said
To unearth presumptions
Of heart and head

If it goes without saying
There's a risk we assume
Our values are shared by
All in the room

If it goes without saying
Let that ring a loud bell
Flag the obvious clearly
As we listen and tell

ODD SOCKS 1

Would it matter to me
Though hidden so none could see
If I wore one sock striped
And the other sock plain white?

Simple logic would show
That the answer should be NO
Could it possibly matter
If hidden socks don't flatter?

But the answer is YES
Though nonsensical I guess
No one would know or care
But all day I'd be aware

Can you tell me, please do
Are you odd sock fussy too?
Do you wear them with pride?
Or in long boots try to hide?

ODD SOCKS 2

Could you be called an odd sock
Not blending in quite right
What you see as black
Others class as white?

I live in the odd sock drawer
Cut deep when I was young
Different in pain
Aching to belong

Red hair framed ugly glasses
Or that is how I thought
Boys could not want me
When would I be sought?

Goody two-shoes shining bright
Serious in studies
Shyness held my tongue
Frozen with new buddies

At school I was outspoken
In friendships sure and true
Stretching out beyond
That I could not do

Shyness lies behind me now
Known for asking questions
Soon as I arrive
Logic ever testing

Find it hard to simply fit
Believe that I belong
Switch analytics off
Follow friendly throng

Odd socks bring their own colours
My poetry and sharing
Writing from the heart
Openly declaring

That all socks bring us beauty
In pairs or on their own
Difference brings pain
And pain to all is known.

VALID

Is the story engrossing
A riveting book

Or is it less painful
Not having to look
At us as we rush past
Engrossed in not looking at you?

Is the dampness depressing
A dreary cold bed

Or is it soul numbing
Just laying your head
On any street pavement
Depressed whether wintry or warm?

Is the future depleted
A bleak hopeless way

Or are you past caring
When taking each day
As it lands itself on you
Depletes you from hoping again?

Are these questions valid
Do they speak to your pain?

Or do they insult as
You sit in the rain
Reading a book that my
Valid life leaves me no time for?

DIRTY WATER

Pedestals cushioned feet of they
Whose call to holy race
Mislead them to embrace
Notions that God's grace
Should or should not be placed
As they decreed

Pedestals custom built for they
Who saw as their sacred quest
The deeming of what was best
For the rest
Of us mere mortals

Pedestals supporting twisted creed
Shielding them
From hunger's bleed
And oozing gash of daily need
Force feeding souls while bodies cry
Hard for us to let it lie
Assigning it to times gone by

Our people no longer need
Look for permission

From men in long cloaks
Who spew of
Tradition
Prohibition
Jaded conditions

Our people now choose
Their path for their lives
Ireland is catching up with the times
Unplugging the deep dark baths of
Filth
Guilt
Tilt
Of human hearts away from kindness

Now digging out the roots of rot
Not a lot
Can be said to excuse
Why our people were trapped in their pain
Shamed
Blamed
Named unworthy
Needing to be told
Not to be bold
Though they were old
Enough to know
Where they wanted to go

Now pouring out those baths of rot
Not a lot
Can be said to excuse
Though we may in mercy say
Those things were of their day
Life was lived that way
Free men enslaved by they
Who held power to shape their lives as clay

Yet as we rush to escape our past
Can we pause in this vital task?
Stop
Reflect
And ask

Are we throwing out
The baby with the bathwater?
Are we cutting off
Our nose to spite our face?
Are we blinded
To gems deep in dirty water?
And bowing to the god of culture's race

NAKED FACE

Would you go outdoors with a naked face
Or only when sheer foundation in place?
Do you spray your legs for an even tan
Or rub till you have bright orange hands?

Will you go natural grey or colour your hair
Do you hate clothes shops
Or feel at home there?
Do you choose your perfume
And stick with one
Or switch and change fragrances
Just for fun?

Do you make the time to paint your nails
With fashion colours from "Off the Rails"?
Would you rather bare hands
Without that fuss
Or a coat of clear varnish if you must?

Do you wear this winter's
Purple and greens
Or throw on whatever matches your jeans?
Is your coat the right length
With fur on your cape
Or do clothes just simply suit your shape?

Thumbs up for good grooming
Ladies fair
Smelling good, looking pretty
Taking care

But when we draw near
Stand in God's grace
We must always approach
With a naked face

SMALL THINGS

Can you see straight through me
To understand just how
I want what I want
And I want it right now

I follow taste again
A moment to enjoy
Guilt whispers in my ear
I drop my head and sigh

Change comes with the small things
That's where we need to win
Seeming unimportant
Yet vital to begin

VANITY

Called to see a friend and have a chat
Walked home with embarrassment

How much I had said
How my words seemed fumbled
How I had not said what I wanted to say

What did it matter anyway?

Let me be focused on my friend
Free from preoccupation of
What might she think of me

Vanity in hidden ways
Looking for my reflection in peoples' eyes

Sent new poems off for friends to read
Read replies with embarrassment

How they might respond
How they might not like them
How they could not say
What they wanted to say

What did it matter anyway?

Let me bring poems from my soul
Free from preoccupation of
What might they think of me

Vanity in hidden ways
Listening for my reflection
In peoples' words

CHAMPAGNE

If I begged for food each day
And my home a cardboard box
Would I want to praise the Lord
And enjoy our daily chats?

If my future life looked bleak
With hard drugs my pressing need
Would I then care who witnessed
About their all loving creed?

If I lived my life in pain
With no hope of any cure
Would I still find it easy
To give worship and adore?

If you read this in prison
Tied by hunger, drugs or pain
And still you truly love God
Then your love is fine champagne

Sparkling rare and vintage stuff
Extravagant and costly
Not based on empty words
Unsure, lukewarm or frosty

The world will search for real faith
Oft ignoring scholar's view
And as they watch your witness
Will ring powerful and true

AGNOSTIC EASTER

I write this on Good Friday
Sitting in a garden splashed with sun
Our bunny hops then stretches
Beneath the shade of hedges
An ant explores a lonely rose
Counting the days
Till flower bud grows
Clothes on washing line
Rustle in a breeze I cannot see
Does this garden understand
In ways unknown to me?

I miss the certainties
My faith of old
That life and its living has bashed to unfold
For now, I can but look and wonder
Take my time and deeply ponder

Indeed, my mind cannot grasp
The height, the depth, the why, the how
So, I have been taught
It would befit me more to bow
As sky above
Below us land or sea
Display God's glorious presence
Leaving no excuse for faithlessness in me

Rocks will cry out
So be wary of doubt
The truth demands I bend my knee
The majesty of God I'm told is plain to see

I was schooled to accept He alone is right
In glory, splendour, Holy might
The Way, The Truth
The One who saves
Who gives pure purpose to life's short days
No one can come to the Father
In any other way
Or so for years, nay decades
I learned to surely say

Now my words are
Maybe
Perhaps
Impossible to know
I can quote Biblical answers
But my heart screams "No"
Where oh where did my deep belief go?

My faith was melted
By the heat of diversity
Tumbled by the torrent of inclusivity

Scattered to the places
Where unanswered questions go
Leaving me with hands full
Of fluorescent "I don't know"

There are folk who know there is no God
There are others who know
God is Lord indeed
More real than reality
Not subject to any man's creed

While they who shake their heads
In disbelief
Appreciate with sadness or relief
Their escape from need to believe or bow
Giving their best to life here and now

I write this on Good Friday
Unsettled by the loss of things
I used to know
Bereaved of belonging to
a God
a Church
a Bible
A faith I could turn to
Where direction would prayerfully show

I yearn to believe in God
But not at any cost
Repulsed by the categories
Saved
Or
Lost

For this agnostic Easter
What will my basket show?
Chocolate stacked amidst whys and hows
And a glaring, fluorescent
I don't know

COLD

Cold creeps in uninvited
Goes first for hands and feet
Climbs up onto the bed
Soaks deep into your sheet

Grabs hold of your nose
Tight it clamps to freeze
Hunts for limbs uncovered
Shoots chills up legs and sleeves

Cold has no manners
Cares not how we feel
Wrap up in many layers
Fight back with heated zeal

MORNING WALK

Cold morning walk
Scarf wrapped tight
Dog sniffs and searches
No one else in sight

Alone with my dog
He knows scandals deep
Woman's trusted confidante
Will all my secrets keep

Sting of sharp breeze
Hat pulled down
Peace of quiet stroll
In sleepy local town

Lights switching on
Breakfast time is near
Deliciousness of silence
My favourite sound to hear

CLAUSTROPHOBIC DARKNESS

Claustrophobic darkness
Rising
Haughtily
Higher

Persistent in desire

Climbs over minutes
Pursuing sweet hours

Relentlessly
Our precious daylight
Devours

CANCELLED PLANS

Joy of cancelled plans
Night by crackling fire
Change into pajamas
Pull the blanket higher

Dust off that novel
Too long on the shelf
Wallow in the free
Time to myself

Or turn on TV show
Watch by fire's glow
Smug to simply know
I can let the evening flow

Or get an early night
Warm in duvet fleece
Either way I'm breathing in
A sigh of deep relief

I did not cancel
This is not on me
Another person takes the wrap
I am guilt free

ELEVEN YEARS

Mam is gone eleven years
It no longer hurts so much
Still Christmas brings refreshing
To the memory of her touch

Her voice
Her smile
Her giggle
We were a giddy pair
Finding humour often
In the midst of aching care

Mam is gone eleven years
Yet I could not
Write this without tears

And Christmas stirs
This pain of mine
Even when I think I'm fine

Let us mind each other
When celebrations make us sad
With feelings sentimental
For the times we might have had

CHRISTMAS IN DECEMBER

October is in autumn
Please give it its day
To trick and treat on local streets
Chase falling leaves with cooling feet
Lost in the season's trance

November starts the winter
Please give it a chance
To have its own rich part to play
Before it must give right of way
To the Christmas dance

December starts the countdown
Please do let us wait
To plan and prep and party much
With family, friends, work and church
Join the Yuletide prance

YEARNING

October evenings fall
Into November ways
December chases close behind
Eager for our praise

With logs in leaping firelight
Clean sprinkling falls of snow
Hot chocolate with marshmallows
Warm house where windows glow

Yes, yes, I hear you
Such comforts light our way
Yet no, the yearning does not stop
For spring with brighter day

DECEMBER TWENTY FIRST

We pass December twenty first
Minute by minute days grow

Shadows of winter pride numbered
Though darkness still seems in full flow

Then bitter days' fall my hope can see
Spring is naughtily waving at me

Let us count down the minutes together
Winter though cruel will not last forever

PONDER THAT

Christmas is what you make it
Mam would always say
Back in the day
I had yet seen nothing
Of the misery it can bring
For they who every year
Must stand alone to sing
Their festive songs
Or sleep on icy footpaths
December 24th
As on every other night
Their bed is made
Of concrete disappointments
As we prepare for lovely surprises

Christmas is what you make it
Let us ponder that

PACKAGE

Sent my parcel
To a certain motel
Best not say the name
Lest it rings alarm bell

Received a message
From said motel
Best go collect
Thinking all would be well

I stood like an eejit
For half an hour
Excitement turning
To feelings sour
This silly machine
With buttons galore
Had me pressing so much
My fingers were sore

I called the office
And made a complaint
My tone neither rude
Nor as sweet as a saint

They listened but could not understand
Why a simple process had got out of hand

Then like a bolt horror struck
What a horrible holy muck
Up I had made
Wasting my day
Having my say
Complaining away

When just up the road
Was my precious load
Exactly where it was meant to be
If I had opened my eyes to see

Hanging my head
In embarrassed shame
I prayed they would
Never remember my name

WRONG SIZE

T'was Christmas Eve
When I realized
The trousers for my hubby
Were in the wrong size

I should have just told him
He would have understood
But no, I took the high way
To be the wifey good

Off I went for shopping
On the craziest of days
Somehow I did manage
To park and find my way

Got the size I wanted
Queued with aching back
Never again will I join in
The Christmas Eve attack

SANTA

Santa no longer stops for me
I'm really very old

His gifts are for the children
Who try to sleep
With eyes shut tight
Wondering what presents
He will bring them tonight

Santa no longer stops for me
I'm really very old

His reindeer cross the night sky
They try to land
On houses bright
Wondering which chimneys
Will be wide or tight

Santa can manage anyhow
The reindeer simply worry
For every Christmas Eve
It seems they are in a hurry

TIME FOR CHRISTMAS SONG

Christmas cards come in the post
Have not yet written mine
Keep saying I will do them
But never make the time
Shopping bags are heavy
To-do list stretches long
Days are growing shorter
When is there time for song?
For carols and for worship
Kneeling at the crib
Forgetting my own worries
And focusing on him
Or bringing him my burdens
And letting him shine light
Believing he still loves me
As he did that Christmas night
When he lay there a baby
No care for self-defense
Glorious High King
Now humbling himself

Such an old, old story
How much of it is true?
Just religious fable
Or life poured out for you?

Christmas cards come in the post
I will write mine today
Activities seem endless
But there'll soon be time for play
For turkey and for stuffing
Chocolates and mulled wine
Watching Christmas movies
Enjoying family time
Your shopping bags are heavy
To-do lists stretching long
But welcome to our service
Today there's time for song

DAYS AFTER CHRISTMAS

These days after Christmas
Throw dark clouds our way
Celebrations done
We are left with bills to pay

Facing into starkness
Of how much money spent
Celebrations over
We are left to pay the rent

Summer's silly days
Seem far out of sight
Celebrations past
We are left to frugal nights

Will we ever learn
To consider future selves
Or always will we fall
For deals on shops' bright shelves

NEW YEAR NEW YOU

Don't get me started
This is a pet hate
Something you hear
So much of late

New Year New You
Was the old you wrong?
No longer skinny enough
To wear, well, a thong

Did the old you run marathons?
The new you certainly must
And while you are doing that
Set up a trust
Or a business
Or write a big book
All the while working hard
On your new look

Whatever you do
Send the old you away
Only new versions
Are welcome to play

BIKINIS

Bikinis in the shops
Just the thing you need
As jeans chafe on the bulge
Expanded by Christmas feed

Itty bitty t-shirts
Skirts that hug your bum
Granny clothes are all that fit
You drive home feeling glum

Slimming clubs start to call your name
Time to face this weighty gain
But first you need some comfort sweet
To soothe your pain with sugary treat

And all because you braved that shop
Next year, safe at home you'll stop

STRESS NOT

Teeny tiny changes
Are the only kind
I have any chance with at all

Take on alterations big
And surely
Soon I am guaranteed to fall

I've tried and tried and tried in desperation
No longer waste my time
In false anticipation

Perhaps there is a tiny thing
That you might change

By this time next year
It might have sprouted

Small changes give us back
Our hope of freedom

At least it's worth a try
I do not doubt it

BRAVADO MOVED OUT

Awaited your reply for many a day
Impatient to read what you would say
Your opinion I longed to hear
As you have been published
And writing for years

Days passed, weeks went by
And without my even having to try
Distracted by life and its lot
I somehow strangely forgot
No longer suspended
In nervous anticipation
No more mind twisting
In guessing or frustration

Remembered then and was proud
My head above the crowd
Glowing to learn I was immune
To how you might sing your tune
No longer straining to hear what you'd say
Secure, independent, blasé

Until that morning
Brought a sudden change of tenant
Triggered by the thought of meeting you
Bravado moved out
Vulnerability rushed in
There was nothing I could do

You mentioned my work
Apologizing for delay
Shocked myself with the words
I then heard my voice say
An instinctive defense
Could not even try
Without premeditation
I started to lie

Telling you I did not mind at all
No, I'd not been waiting
I'd been having a ball
With life and all its traits
I'd not noticed that you'd made me wait

Did you see through me then?
You looked surprised
Could you feel me cringe
Through a silly disguise?
You know how it feels
To pour your heart out
And try not to care how it's heard
The more I spoke
The more I wished
To take back foolish words

Considered simple honesty
Wanted the truth to be told
Backtracking would have embarrassed
And pride had too strong a hold

Found myself straining
To hear what you'd say
Good-bye to secure
And farewell to blasé

Author's Note

Thank you again for reading my poetry. I hope the words resonated with you.

Love Sandra

Printed in Great Britain
by Amazon